PETS IN TRUMPETS

and other word-play riddles

by Bernard Most

HARCOURT BRACE JOVANOVICH, PUBLISHERS

San Diego   New York   London

The following **pages** are dedicated to readers of all **ages**.

Copyright © 1991 by Bernard Most

Requests for permission to make copies of any
part of the work should be mailed to:
Permissions Department, Harcourt Brace Jovanovich, Publishers,
Orlando, Florida 32887.

Library of Congress Cataloging-in-Publication Data

Most, Bernard.
Pets in trumpets/by Bernard Most. — 1st ed.
p.   cm.
Summary: Fifteen word-play riddles based on the concept of finding
words within other words, such as "pet" in "trumpet" and "ten" in
"kitten."
ISBN 0-15-261210-6
1. Riddles, Juvenile. 2. Wit and humor, Juvenile. [1. Riddles.
2. Vocabulary.] I. Title.
PN6371.5.M63   1991
818′.5402 — dc20   90-23873

Printed in Singapore

First edition

A B C D E

Why did the musician find a dog in his **trumpet**?

Because he always finds a

pet

in his trum<u>pet</u>.

What kind of **ghost** invites you into its haunted house?

A g<u>host</u> that is a good

host.

Why were the

mice

invited to the picnic?

Because the m<u>ice</u> brought the

ice.

What happens when a greedy
gorilla
eats too many bananas?

The greedy gorilla gets ill.

Why should you keep a polar bear off your **furniture**?

So you won't get

fur

on your <u>fur</u>niture.

What makes a city **street** more colorful?

A
tree
makes a city s<u>tree</u>t more colorful.

Why did the
witch
let children hold her broomstick?

Because the <u>witch</u> had a very bad

itch.

What can you find **thousands** of at the beach?

You can find thousands of grains of **sand**.

Why is the **dragon** trying to lift its tail off the ground?

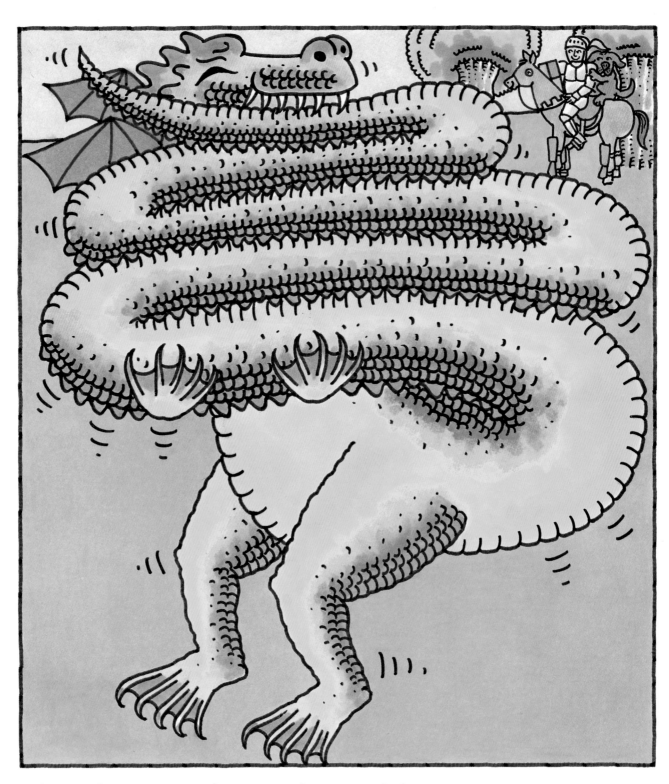

The <u>drag</u>on doesn't want to

drag

it around anymore.

Who would always be ready to
share
your carrots?

A hungry

hare

would always be ready to s<u>hare</u>.

What do you give a newly

hatched

bald eagle?

You give a newly <u>hat</u>ched bald eagle a

hat.

How did the monkey get in the house?

The mon<u>key</u> got in with a
key.

What does an artistic

weasel

need?

An artistic w<u>easel</u> needs an

easel.

How many
kittens
are in a big family?

There are

ten

kit<u>te</u>ns in this big family.

What did the dog find in the

trombone?

He finally found his

bone

in the trom<u>bone</u>.